ESSENTIALS
FOR CHRISTIAN LIVING

———————○———————

PRAYERS AND TRUTHS OF THE CATHOLIC CHURCH
WITH SPACE FOR PERSONAL REFLECTION

Msgr. Pietro Principe

WHAT PROFIT WOULD THERE BE FOR ONE
TO GAIN THE WHOLE WORLD
AND FORFEIT HIS LIFE?
(MT 16:26)

Libreria Editrice Vaticana

United States Conference of Catholic Bishops
Washington, D.C.

Photos: cover, p. i, Tom Grill/Corbis.

First printing, February 2008
Second printing, September 2011

Printed in the United States of America
ISBN 978-1-60137-020-4
USCCB Communictions
3211 Fourth Street, NE
Washington, DC 20017-1194
www.usccbpublishing.org

CONTENTS

NOTE

As an aid to additional personal study, *Essentials for Catholic Living* refers regularly to the *Catechism of the Catholic Church* (CCC) and the *Compendium of the Catechism of the Catholic Church* ("*Compendium*").

Most prayers are taken from the *Compendium of the Catechism of the Catholic Church*; others are taken from the *Manual of Indulgences* and *Catholic Household Blessings and Prayers* (revised edition). Scripture texts used in this work are taken from the *New American Bible*.

INTRODUCTION

he purpose of *Essentials for Christian Living* is to recall in summary form what Catholics must know and put into practice.

In the **first part** the traditional prayers and formulas of Catholic doctrine are presented.

In the **second part** the basic pillars of the faith—the Creed, sacraments, and commandments—are explained according to what is set forth in the *Catechism of the Catholic Church* (CCC).

An additional special feature of *Essentials for Christian Living* is the blank space found on each page. It is an invitation:

- To pause for a moment of inner silence
- To focus one's attention
- To write down a thought
- To draw a picture
- To formulate a resolution
- To recall an example
- To highlight a key word
- To reflect on the text in the style of *lectio divina*

PART I

I n this first part of *Essentials for Christian Living*, the **prayers** of the Catholic Tradition are presented. Some of these go back to the very earliest ages of the Church, when Christians were still being persecuted. Others have developed out of the lived faith of individuals and communities who were specially inspired by the Holy Spirit.

This part also sets forth the **formulas** of Catholic doctrine, to serve as a memory aid for believers.

PRAYERS

"For where two or three are gathered together in my name, there am I in the midst of them" (Mt 18:20).

"All these devoted themselves with one accord to prayer, together with some women, and Mary the mother of Jesus" (Acts 1:14).

"It is the *heart* that prays. If our heart is far from God, the words of prayer are in vain" (CCC, no. 2562).

THE SIGN OF THE CROSS

In the name of the Father
and of the Son
and of the Holy Spirit. Amen.

he Sign of the Cross, which recalls how Christ redeemed us, has accompanied Christianity since the beginning. It was traced on the forehead with a finger of the right hand. The first Christians often used this sign at the beginning of the day, upon entering or leaving their house, or before facing martyrdom.

The large Sign of the Cross—in which the right hand moves from the forehead to the lower part of the chest, and from the left shoulder to the right—has been used since the fifth to sixth century.

"We make the Sign of the Cross before prayer in order to recollect and compose ourselves spiritually, and to focus our thoughts, heart, and will upon God. We make it after prayer so that God's gifts might remain in us. We make it in temptation, to find strength; in danger, to be protected. It is made when giving blessings so that the fullness of God's life might penetrate the soul. . . . Do it properly. Take your time, make a large cross, think of what you are doing" (Romano Guardini).

Our Father

Our Father who art in heaven,
hallowed be thy name.
Thy kingdom come.
Thy will be done on earth, as it is
in heaven.
Give us this day our daily bread,
and forgive us our trespasses,
    as we forgive those who trespass
    against us,
and lead us not into temptation,
but deliver us from evil.

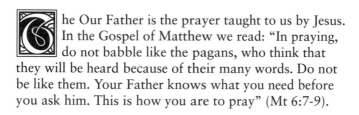he Our Father is the prayer taught to us by Jesus. In the Gospel of Matthew we read: "In praying, do not babble like the pagans, who think that they will be heard because of their many words. Do not be like them. Your Father knows what you need before you ask him. This is how you are to pray" (Mt 6:7-9).

In reciting the Our Father, we give glory to God. We ask him for our needs and for forgiveness of our sins. For an entire night, St. Francis of Assisi was heard saying over and over: "My Father, my All." Love does not need to use many words!

"My Father, I abandon myself to you; do with me what you will. Whatever you may do with me, I thank you. I am ready for all, I accept all, provided only that your will be done in me and in all your creatures . . ." (Blessed Charles de Foucauld).

GLORY BE TO THE FATHER

Glory be to the Father
and to the Son
and to the Holy Spirit,
as it was in the beginning
is now, and ever shall be
world without end. Amen.

he Glory Be to the Father, a formula of praise to the three Persons of the blessed Trinity, is a simple development of the trinitarian baptismal formula: "Go, therefore, and make disciples of all nations, baptizing them in the name of the Father, and of the Son, and of the holy Spirit" (Mt 28:19).

We do not know exactly who its author was or when it was introduced into the liturgy. The second part was added in the fourth century. It is historically certain that it was in regular use at the time of St. Benedict (during the fifth to sixth century).

Believers can use the invocation as a profession of faith.

THE CREED

I believe in God the Father almighty,
    Creator of heaven and earth.
And in Jesus Christ, his only Son, our
    Lord, who was conceived by the
    Holy Spirit,
born of the Virgin Mary, suffered
    under Pontius Pilate,
was crucified, died, and was buried.
He descended into hell; the third day
    he rose again from the dead;

He ascended into heaven, and sits at
the right hand of God the Father
almighty, from thence he shall
come to judge the living and
the dead.
I believe in the Holy Spirit, the holy
Catholic Church, the communion
of saints, the forgiveness of sins, the
resurrection of the body and life
everlasting. Amen.

he Creed is the oldest catechism, used by the Church from the beginning.

"It is also customary to reckon the articles of the Creed as *twelve*, thus symbolizing the fullness of the apostolic faith by the number of the apostles" (CCC, no. 191).

"To say the Credo [Creed] with faith is to enter into communion with God, Father, Son, and Holy Spirit" (CCC, no. 197).

In addition to the Apostles' Creed, we recite the Niceno-Constantinopolitan (or Nicene) Creed, which remains common to all the great Churches of both East and West to this day (see CCC, no. 195).

COME, CREATOR SPIRIT
(VENI, CREATOR SPIRITUS)

Come, Holy Spirit, Creator come,
From your bright heavenly throne!
Come, take possession of our souls,
And make them all your own.
You who are called the Paraclete,
Best gift of God above,
The living spring, the living fire,
Sweet unction, and true love!
You who are sevenfold in your grace,
Finger of God's right hand,

His promise, teaching little ones
To speak and understand!
O guide our minds with your
  blessed light,
With love our hearts inflame,
And with your strength which
  never decays
Confirm our mortal frame.
Far from us drive our hellish foe
True peace unto us bring,
And through all perils guide us safe

Beneath your sacred wing.
Through you may we the
   Father know,
Through you the eternal Son
And you the Spirit of them both
Thrice-blessed three in one.
All glory to the Father be,
And to the Risen Son;
The same to you, O Paraclete,
While endless ages run. Amen.

evotion to the Holy Spirit is the most important expression of Christian piety. Without his help we cannot even say the name of Jesus (see 1 Cor 12:3). In the Apostles' Creed we say, "I believe in the Holy Spirit." Through him was accomplished the greatest work of God's love: the Incarnation of the Word by Mary. How moving is the hymn of the Church that begs him, "Come, Creator Spirit."

St. Paul, in his Letter to the Galatians (5:22), lists the fruits of the Holy Spirit: love, joy, peace, patience, kindness, generosity, faithfulness, gentleness, and self-control. Thus, the Spirit creates in us an openness to both God and neighbor. The Spirit gives us the ability to bear witness to Christ by the practice of charity. It is no accident that many hospitals in the Middle Ages were named after the Holy Spirit. Moreover, the term "Paraclete," which is ascribed to the Holy Spirit, means "Consoler," or one who gives aid.

THE HAIL MARY

Hail, Mary, full of grace,
the Lord is with thee.
Blessed art thou among women
and blessed is the fruit of thy
    womb, Jesus.

Holy Mary, Mother of God,
pray for us sinners,
now and at the hour of our death.
Amen.

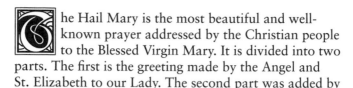he Hail Mary is the most beautiful and well-known prayer addressed by the Christian people to the Blessed Virgin Mary. It is divided into two parts. The first is the greeting made by the Angel and St. Elizabeth to our Lady. The second part was added by the Church.

The central word is "Jesus," showing that the Mother's greatness rests in that of her Son. This idea is well expressed by Dante in *Paradiso* XXXIII where, through the mouth of St. Bernard, he calls her "daughter of your Son."

In the Hail Mary we greet our Lady and ask her to obtain forgiveness of our sins and a happy death.

HAIL, HOLY QUEEN
(SALVE REGINA)

Hail, Holy Queen, Mother of Mercy,
our life, our sweetness and our hope.
To thee do we cry,
poor banished children of Eve.
To thee do we send up our sighs,
mourning and weeping in this valley
    of tears.
Turn then, most gracious advocate,
thine eyes of mercy toward us,

and after this exile
show unto us the blessed fruit of thy
    womb, Jesus.
O clement, O loving,
O sweet Virgin Mary.

his is one of the best-known prayers of the Christian Tradition. It is the sigh of a pilgrim on the way to the homeland, who feels the need for firm support for the journey. In reciting the Hail, Holy Queen, our spirit is refreshed, and our heart begins to trust in the "Mother of Mercy."

The authorship of the Hail, Holy Queen is uncertain. While it is no longer attributed to St. Bernard, the antiphon has been used daily by the Cistercians in their recitation of the Liturgy of the Hours since the middle of the twelfth century.

The expression "Mother of Mercy" was a favorite one in Benedictine spirituality.

The Angelus

V. The Angel of the Lord declared
unto Mary.
R. And she conceived of the
Holy Spirit.
Hail, Mary . . .

V. Behold the handmaid of the Lord.
R. Be it done unto me according to
thy word.
Hail, Mary . . .

V. And the Word was made flesh.

R. And dwelt among us.

Hail, Mary . . .

V. Pray for us, O holy Mother of God.

R. That we may be made worthy of the promises of Christ.

Let us pray:

Pour forth, we beseech thee, O Lord, thy grace into our hearts; that we, to whom the Incarnation of Christ, thy Son, was made known by the message of an angel, may by his

Passion and Cross be brought to the glory of his Resurrection. Through the same Christ, our Lord. Amen.

or many centuries Christian piety has loved to recall (in the morning, at noon, and in the evening) the mystery of the Incarnation of the Son of God, while at the same time praising Mary as Mother of Christ and of humanity.

This devotion began before the tenth century in a church in Saintes (France), where the faithful were summoned to recite the prayer by the sound of the bell.

Pope Urban II († 1099) is said to have ordered it at the Council of Clermont, to implore Mary's help for the armies that were fighting against the Turks (1095).

It is well documented that St. Bonaventure († 1274) urged his friars to promote this pious practice among the faithful.

THE ROSARY

God, come to my assistance.
  Lord, make haste to help me.

Glory be to the Father. . . .

O my Jesus, forgive us our sins, save
us from the fires of hell;
lead all souls to Heaven, especially
those who have most need of
your mercy.

STRUCTURE OF EACH DECADE:

- Mention of the mystery
- Short pause for meditation
- Our Father
- Hail Mary (ten times)
- Glory Be

THE JOYFUL MYSTERIES

(recited Monday and Saturday)
1. The Annunciation
2. The Visitation
3. The Nativity
4. The Presentation
5. The Finding in the Temple

THE MYSTERIES OF LIGHT

(recited Thursday)

1. The Baptism of Jesus
2. The Wedding Feast of Cana
3. The Proclamation of the Kingdom, with the call to Conversion
4. The Transfiguration
5. The Institution of the Eucharist

THE SORROWFUL MYSTERIES

(recited Tuesday and Friday)

1. The Agony in the Garden
2. The Scourging at the Pillar
3. The Crowning with Thorns
4. The Carrying of the Cross
5. The Crucifixion

THE GLORIOUS MYSTERIES

(recited Wednesday and Sunday)
1. The Resurrection
2. The Ascension
3. The Descent of the Holy Spirit
4. The Assumption
5. The Coronation of Mary Queen of Heaven and Earth

Prayer Concluding the Rosary
Hail, Holy Queen, etc., as on p. 21.

V. Pray for us, O holy Mother of God.
R. That we may be made worthy of the promises of Christ.

Let us pray.

O God, whose only-begotten Son, by his life, death and resurrection, has purchased for us the rewards of eternal life, grant, we beseech thee, that meditating on these mysteries of the most holy Rosary of the Blessed Virgin Mary, we may imitate what they contain and obtain what they promise, through the same Christ our Lord. Amen.

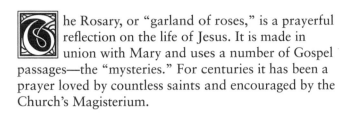

he Rosary, or "garland of roses," is a prayerful reflection on the life of Jesus. It is made in union with Mary and uses a number of Gospel passages—the "mysteries." For centuries it has been a prayer loved by countless saints and encouraged by the Church's Magisterium.

Many events are linked to Mary and her recommendation to recite the Rosary. These are truly marvelous events.

John Paul II brought in the Rosary's Christological dimension by adding the Mysteries of Light, which focus on episodes in the life of Christ. Now we have even greater reason to say that the Rosary is a compendium of the Gospel.

ETERNAL REST

Eternal rest grant unto them, O Lord,
and let perpetual light shine
　　upon them.
May they rest in peace.
Amen.

ternal Rest (*Requiem aeternam*) is an ancient prayer asking God to grant rest, peace, and eternal happiness to the souls of the faithful departed by giving them the joy of paradise.

Since the time of the first Christian catacombs, the Church has prayed for the dead and remembered them in the celebration of the Eucharist.

Paradise, which is eternal union with God, does not mean isolation. It is based on a perfect "communion of saints," since in Christ the living intercede for the dead and the dead intercede for the living.

Angel of God

Angel of God, my guardian dear,
to whom God's love commits me here,
ever this day be at my side,
to light and guard, to rule and guide.
Amen.

ngel of God, a brief synthesis of ancient prayers, is an expression of the Christian people's devotion to guardian angels.

In his Rule, St. Benedict reminds the monks that the Divine Office is recited in the presence of God and the angels. St. Thomas Aquinas says that every person, from the moment of birth, is given an angel.

"The existence of the spiritual, non-corporeal beings that Sacred Scripture usually calls 'angels' is a truth of faith" (CCC, no. 328).

Act of Faith

O my God, I firmly believe that you
are one God in three divine Persons,
Father, Son, and Holy Spirit. I believe
that your divine Son became man
and died for our sins and that he
will come to judge the living and
the dead. I believe these and all
the truths which the Holy Catholic
Church teaches because you have
revealed them who are eternal
truth and wisdom, who can neither
deceive nor be deceived. In this faith
I intend to live and die. Amen.

he Act of Faith—together with the Acts of Hope, Love, and Contrition—appeared as a catechetical formula at the beginning of the nineteenth century. The French Revolution (1789) had shocked the world and given birth to an age hostile to Revelation. These formulas, which became part of the Tradition and have come down to our own day, sprang up in order to provide direction for believers.

The Act of Faith is an expression of the believer's commitment. The certainty of faith surpasses all doubts and conveys trust in God and in the Church.

ACT OF HOPE

O Lord God, I hope by your grace for the pardon of all my sins and after life here to gain eternal happiness because you have promised it who are infinitely powerful, faithful, kind, and merciful. In this hope I intend to live and die. Amen.

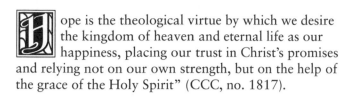ope is the theological virtue by which we desire the kingdom of heaven and eternal life as our happiness, placing our trust in Christ's promises and relying not on our own strength, but on the help of the grace of the Holy Spirit" (CCC, no. 1817).

In opposition to the eighteenth-century Enlightenment, which thought it could solve all of human society's problems by the light of reason alone, prescinding from God, Christianity offers a hope that does not deceive. "My God, I hope," means "My God, I expect with certainty." Dante spoke of "the certain expectation."

ACT OF LOVE

O Lord God, I love you above all
things and I love my neighbor for
your sake because you are the
highest, infinite and perfect good,
worthy of all my love. In this love I
intend to live and die. Amen.

t a moment in history marked by hatred, terror, violence, and war (as was the case in the early nineteenth century) the Church repeats Christ's new commandment: "This is my commandment: love one another as I love you" (Jn 15:12).

So it was that in the early nineteenth century, many religious congregations sprang up, especially women's congregations, whose charism was to perform works of charity.

"By charity, we love God above all things and our neighbor as ourselves for love of God. Charity, the form of all the virtues, 'binds everything together in perfect harmony' (Col 3:14)" (CCC, no. 1844).

Act of Contrition

O my God, I am heartily sorry for having offended Thee, and I detest all my sins because of thy just punishments, but most of all because they offend Thee, my God, who art all good and deserving of all my love. I firmly resolve with the help of Thy grace to sin no more and to avoid the near occasion of sin. Amen.

epent, and believe in the gospel" (Mk 1:15).

"There is no offense, however serious, that the Church cannot forgive. 'There is no one, however wicked and guilty, who may not confidently hope for forgiveness, provided his repentance is honest.' Christ who died for all men desires that in his Church the gates of forgiveness should always be open to anyone who turns away from sin" (CCC, no. 982).

In the Act of Contrition, Christians ask for pardon from God for sins committed, certain that they must "never despair of God's mercy" (Rule of St. Benedict).

MORNING PRAYER

O my God, I adore you.
I love you with all my heart.
I thank you for creating me,
making me a Christian,
and protecting me throughout
   the night.
I offer you my actions today;
may they all be according to your
   holy will
and for your greater glory.

Keep me from sin
and from every evil.
May your grace
always be with me
and with all who are dear to me.
Amen.

t the beginning of a new day it is natural to turn our thoughts to God in order to thank him, adore him, and entrust ourselves to him.

The shadows of the night now fade;
the light of dawn shines radiantly.
We lift our hearts and minds in prayer
to God the Almighty.
(Liturgy of the Hours)

Praised be you, my Lord, with all your creatures,
especially Sir Brother Sun,
who is the day and through whom you give us light.
And he is beautiful and radiant with great splendor;
and bears a likeness of you, Most High One.
(from the Canticle of the Sun by St. Francis)

Evening Prayer

O my God, I adore you.
I love you with all my heart.
I thank you for creating me,
making me a Christian,
and protecting me throughout
   this day.
Forgive the sins
I have committed today,
and if I have accomplished any good,
accept it.

Watch over me as I sleep,
and free me from danger.
May your grace
always be with me
and with all who are dear to me.
Amen.

he evening, before we take our night's rest, is the time to thank God and to reflect on the mystery of life and death.

Before the twilight fades away,
Creator of the world, we pray
that you, in your great mercy, might
protect and guard us through the night.
(Liturgy of the Hours)

"Everything we are and have comes from [God]: 'What have you that you did not receive?' (1 Cor 4:7)" (CCC, no. 224).

INVOCATIONS

- Lord, hear my prayer.
- My Jesus, mercy.
- My God and my all.
- Lord, have mercy on me, a sinner.
- Lord, increase my faith.
- Lord, help my unbelief.
- My God, I love you.
- Lord, your will be done.
- Your kingdom come!
- My Lord and my God.
- Blessed be God!

- Jesus, Mary and Joseph, I give you my heart and my soul.
  Jesus, Mary and Joseph, assist me in my last agony.
  Jesus, Mary and Joseph, may I breathe forth my soul in peace with you.
- May the most holy and divine Sacrament be blessed and praised now and forever.
- Heart of Jesus, burning with love for us, inflame our hearts with love for you.
- Heart of Jesus, I trust in you.
- Lord, you know all things; you know that I love you.

- Divine heart of Jesus: convert sinners, save the dying, free the holy souls in purgatory.
- Sweet heart of Jesus, I implore that I may love you more and more.
- Sweet heart of Mary, be my salvation.
- Lord, show me your mercy, and grant me your salvation.
- Lord, send out your Spirit, and renew the face of the earth.
- Come, Holy Spirit, come!
  And from your heavenly home
  Shed a ray of light divine!
- Mary, my mother, my hope.

- Grant us continual health of mind and body, O Virgin Mary.
- Mother of our Savior, pray for us who have recourse to you.
- Jesus, Mary, Joseph.
- Watch over your Church, Lord.
- Lord, give to those who have died the joy of paradise.
- Lord, protect all travelers.
- Comfort the aged, O Lord.
- Lord, fill the young with enthusiasm in their journey to you.
- Thanks be to God.

nvocations are short prayers, repetitive but penetrating. They are a movement of the heart toward God, toward the Blessed Virgin Mary, toward the saints. They may be compared to a phone call to someone we love to say hello, to share a memory, to ask for help.

They do not require any time and can be inserted into the other activities that occupy us ("Pray and work").

In moments of distress, difficulty, or depression, or in moments of joy and peace, they are an effective way to remain united with God.

Concerning the invocation "Thanks be to God," St. Augustine writes in one of his letters that it is impossible to say anything more brief, more joyful, more grand, or more efficacious.

THE WAY OF THE CROSS

Before each station:

Leader: We adore you, O Christ,
and we bless you.

All: Because by your holy Cross
you have redeemed the world.

After each station:

Lord Jesus, help us walk in your
steps. [Lord Jesus crucified, have
mercy on us.]

First Station: Jesus is condemned
to death

Second Station: Jesus takes up
his Cross

Third Station: Jesus falls the
first time

Fourth Station: Jesus meets
his mother

Fifth Station: Simon of Cyrene
helps Jesus

Sixth Station: Veronica wipes the
face of Jesus

Seventh Station: Jesus falls a
second time

Eighth Station: Jesus speaks to the
women of Jerusalem

Ninth Station: Jesus falls the
   third time
Tenth Station: Jesus is stripped of
   his clothes
Eleventh Station: Jesus is nailed
   to the Cross
Twelfth Station: Jesus dies
   on the Cross
Thirteenth Station: Jesus is
   removed from the Cross
Fourteenth Station: Jesus is placed
   in the tomb

- Jesus is raised from the dead

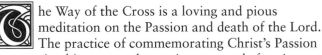

he Way of the Cross is a loving and pious meditation on the Passion and death of the Lord. The practice of commemorating Christ's Passion by retracing his steps and stopping to pray before images of the various episodes that are the subjects of meditation was brought to Europe by pilgrims returning from the Holy Land.

It consists of fourteen stations. The first one to introduce these is thought to have been the Dominican Blessed Alvaro († 1420). The Franciscans, especially St. Leonard of Port Maurice († 1751), established and popularized it.

The Way of the Cross is one of the most effective ways for the faithful to rediscover in the stations—which are filled with so much sorrow and compassion—a way to turn from sin to a Christian life.

Popes Innocent XI, Innocent XII, Benedict XII, and Benedict XIV enriched the Way of the Cross with many indulgences.

Prayer to St. Joseph

St. Joseph, chosen by God to be the most pure spouse of Mary and the foster father of Jesus, pray for us who have recourse to you. You who were the faithful guardian of the Holy Family, bless and protect our family and all Christian families. You who experienced trials, labor, and fatigue in your life, help all who work and all who suffer. You who were given the grace to die in the arms of Jesus and Mary, assist and comfort all who

are sick and dying. You who are
the patron of the Church, intercede
for the pope, the bishops, and all
the faithful throughout the world,
especially those who are oppressed
or suffer persecution for the name of
Christ. Amen.

oseph is the last patriarch to receive messages from God in the humble form of dreams. Like the Joseph of old, he is the righteous and faithful one (Mt 1:19) whom God made guardian of his household. He links Jesus, the messianic King, to the descendants of David. Husband of Mary and foster father, he guides the Holy Family as it flees to Egypt and then returns, retracing the journey of the Exodus. Pius IX declared him patron of the Universal Church, and John XXIII inserted his name into the Roman Canon" (from the *Roman Missal*).

"Saint Joseph's silence does not express an inner emptiness but, on the contrary, the fullness of the faith [which] he bears in his heart and which guides his every thought and action" (Pope Benedict XVI, Angelus, December 18, 2005).

AMEN

The adverb "Amen" derives from a Hebrew root meaning firmness, certainty, security, or acceptance of something as true. Thus, "Amen" means "So it is" or "Truly." Later it would come to mean "So be it."

In Christian worship, at almost every moment, this Hebrew word is used because it is more forceful than any translation. To say "Amen" means to proclaim that we hold what has been said to be true. By it we ratify a statement or unite ourselves to a prayer.

In the early days it served to ratify the election of bishops. Thus, around AD 430, when St. Augustine proposed to the faithful that Heraclius be his successor, they accepted by responding over and over, "Amen, Amen."

Dante places this word on the lips of the Blessed in heaven (*Paradiso* XIV, 62).

THE MASS

The Mass is the supreme act of worship of the Christian people.

Therefore, it is necessary that the reality of the Eucharist be given special emphasis, as it has had in Christian tradition since the first centuries: "The celebration of Mass, the action of Christ and the people of God arrayed hierarchically, is the center of the whole Christian life for the Church both universal and local, as well as for each of the faithful individually" (*General Instruction of the Roman Missal*, no. 16).

WHAT IS THE MASS?

The inexhaustible richness of the Mass is expressed by the different names we give it, which evoke particular aspects (see CCC, nos. 1328ff.): Eucharist, the Lord's Supper, memorial of the Lord's death and Resurrection, breaking of the bread, Holy Sacrifice, Eucharistic celebration, most Blessed Sacrament, etc.

The *Catechism of the Catholic Church* says, "The Mass is at the same time, and inseparably, the sacrificial memorial in which the sacrifice of the cross is perpetuated and the sacred banquet of communion with the Lord's body and blood" (no. 1382).

"The Mass is made up, as it were, of two parts: the Liturgy of the Word and the Liturgy of the Eucharist. These, however, are so closely interconnected that they form but one single act of worship. For in the Mass the table both of God's word and of Christ's body is prepared, from which the faithful may be instructed and refreshed" (*General Instruction of the Roman Missal*, no. 28).

THE STRUCTURE OF THE MASS

Every Mass has a common structure. The two parts are usually subdivided as follows:

1. *Introductory Rites*

The rites preceding the Liturgy of the Word—namely the Entrance, Greeting, Act of Penitence, *Kyrie*, *Gloria*, and Collect—are a preparation for listening to God's Word and celebrating the Eucharist worthily.

2. Liturgy of the Word

The readings from Sacred Scripture (two on weekdays, three on festive days), homily, Profession of Faith, and Prayer of the Faithful recall that Christ is present through his Word in the community that participates in the rite.

3. Liturgy of the Eucharist

With the Eucharistic liturgy, we come to the heart of the celebration. The priest, in carrying out the Eucharistic liturgy, acts *in persona Christi*, in the person of Christ. The faithful participate by bringing to the altar bread and wine with water—the same elements Christ took in his hands in the act of instituting the Sacrament of the Eucharist. Then the celebrant associates the whole assembly with himself in the prayer addressed to the Father (the Eucharistic Prayer, in all its parts, is always addressed to the Father) and carries out what the Lord himself did at the Last Supper: the memorial of his death and Resurrection. The chief elements of the Eucharistic Prayer are Thanksgiving (Preface), Acclamation (*Sanctus*), Epiclesis (prayer to the Father to send the Holy Spirit), the account of Jesus' Last Supper, the Consecration (in which the Body and Blood of Christ are made sacramentally present), the Anamnesis (memorial of the Passion and

Resurrection), offering of the bread of life and the cup of salvation, the intercessions of the whole Church, and the Doxology (an act of glorification and praise by the community).

4. Communion Rite

The Communion rite is introduced by the recitation of the Our Father and includes the prayers of preparation for the Paschal Banquet, the sign of peace, the communion of the celebrant and the people, and thanksgiving.

5. Concluding Rites

The greeting and final blessing dismiss the Assembly.

THE MASS: LIFE OF THE CHRISTIAN COMMUNITY

"If from the beginning Christians have celebrated the Eucharist . . . it is because we know ourselves to be bound by the command the Lord gave on the eve of his Passion: 'Do this in remembrance of me' (1 Cor 11:24-25)" (CCC, no. 1356).

The words of the Mass should inspire in all a missionary drive. Kierkegaard, in his *Diary*, has left us this thought: "Is it lawful to receive Communion without devoting ourselves to the apostolate, even to the point of martyrdom?"

The Mass must be lived every day, faithfully and consistently. "The Mass, well celebrated, spreads its perfume over the whole day" (John XXIII).

One way to know and live the Mass is through use of a missal, which should be in the hands of every believer.

THE MASS THROUGH THE AGES

"The Eucharist is 'the source and summit of the Christian life'" (CCC, no. 1324, citing *Lumen Gentium*, no. 11).

As the golden thread (see CCC, no. 1345ff.) that accompanies the Church of the apostles, the Church of the catacombs, the Church of the martyrs, and the Church of the saints, the Mass testifies until the present day that "those who receive the Eucharist are united more closely to Christ" (CCC, no. 1396).

From a book that goes back to the Middle Ages, a book that Bossuet († 1704) was able to call "the fifth Gospel," a book esteemed even by Voltaire († 1728), we cite the following page on the Eucharist:

> I feel there are especially necessary for me in this life two things without which its miseries would be unbearable. Confined here in this prison of the body I confess I need these two, food and light. Therefore, You have given me in my weakness Your sacred Flesh to refresh my soul and body, and You have set Your word as the guiding light for my feet. Without them I could not live aright, for the word of God is the light of my soul and Your Sacrament is the Bread of Life. These also may be called the two tables, one here, one there, in the treasure house of holy Church. (from the *Imitation of Christ*)

FORMULAS OF CATHOLIC DOCTRINE

eaven and earth will pass away, but my words will not pass away" (Mk 13:31).

The formulas summarize the essential content of the truths of faith. Expressed in a brief yet compact form, they help recall the fixed points in the life of a Christian. They may appear to be dry, but in fact they refer to the one center that is Christ.

The Principal
Mysteries of Faith

1. The Unity and Trinity of God
2. The Incarnation, Passion, Death, and Resurrection of our Lord Jesus Christ

(see CCC, nos. 234, 483)

THE TWO COMMANDMENTS OF LOVE

1. You shall love the Lord your God with all your heart, with all your soul, and with all your mind.
2. You shall love your neighbor as yourself.

(*Compendium*, p. 192 [Appendix B], quoting Mt 22:37-40)

THE GOLDEN RULE

"Do to others whatever you would have them do to you. This is the law and the prophets" (Mt 7:12).

THE SEVEN SACRAMENTS

1. Baptism
2. Confirmation or Chrismation
3. Eucharist
4. Penance or Reconciliation
5. Anointing of the Sick
6. Holy Orders
7. Matrimony

(see CCC, no. 1113)

THE TEN COMMANDMENTS

1. I am the LORD your God: you shall not have strange gods before me.
2. You shall not take the name of the LORD your God in vain.
3. Remember to keep holy the LORD's Day.
4. Honor your father and your mother.
5. You shall not kill.

6. You shall not commit adultery.
7. You shall not steal.
8. You shall not bear false witness against your neighbor.
9. You shall not covet your neighbor's wife.
10. You shall not covet your neighbor's goods.

(see CCC, nos. 2051, 2052)

THE THREE
THEOLOGICAL VIRTUES

1. Faith
2. Hope
3. Charity

(*Compendium*, p. 192 [Appendix B]; see CCC, nos. 1814, 1817, 1822)

THE FOUR CARDINAL VIRTUES

1. Prudence
2. Justice
3. Fortitude
4. Temperance

(*Compendium*, p. 192 [Appendix B]; see CCC, nos. 1805-1809)

THE SEVEN GIFTS OF THE HOLY SPIRIT

1. Wisdom
2. Understanding
3. Counsel
4. Fortitude
5. Knowledge
6. Piety
7. Fear of the Lord

(*Compendium*, p. 192 [Appendix B]; see CCC, no. 1830)

THE GOSPEL BEATITUDES

Blessed are the poor in spirit,
  for theirs is the kingdom of heaven.
Blessed are they who mourn,
  for they will be comforted.
Blessed are the meek,
  for they will inherit the earth.
Blessed are they who hunger and
  thirst for righteousness,
  for they will be satisfied.
Blessed are the merciful,
  for they will be shown mercy.
Blessed are the pure of heart,
  for they will see God.

Blessed are the peacemakers,
>for they will be called children
>of God.

Blessed are those who are persecuted
>for righteousness' sake,
>for theirs is the kingdom
>of heaven.

Blessed are you when people revile
>you and persecute you and utter
>all kinds of evil against you falsely
>on my account.

Rejoice and be glad,
>for your reward will be great
>in heaven.

(*Compendium*, p. 192 [Appendix B]; see
Mt 5:3-12)

THE FOUR LAST THINGS

1. Death
2. Judgment
3. Hell
4. Heaven

(*Compendium*, p. 193 [Appendix B]; see CCC, nos. 1020, 1025, 1033, 1040)

THE SEVEN CAPITAL SINS

1. Pride
2. Covetousness
3. Lust
4. Anger
5. Gluttony
6. Envy
7. Sloth

(*Compendium*, p. 193 [Appendix B]; see CCC, no. 1876)

THE SEVEN SPIRITUAL WORKS OF MERCY

1. Counsel the doubtful.
2. Instruct the ignorant.
3. Admonish sinners.
4. Comfort the afflicted.
5. Forgive offenses.
6. Bear wrongs patiently.
7. Pray for the living and the dead.

(*Compendium*, p. 193 [Appendix B]; see CCC, no. 2447)

THE SEVEN CORPORAL WORKS OF MERCY

1. Feed the hungry.
2. Give drink to the thirsty.
3. Clothe the naked.
4. Shelter the homeless.
5. Visit the sick.
6. Visit the imprisoned.
7. Bury the dead.

(*Compendium*, p. 193 [Appendix B]; see CCC, no. 2447)

THE FIVE PRECEPTS OF THE CHURCH

1. You shall attend Mass on Sundays and on holy days of obligation and remain free from work or activity that could impede the sanctification of such days.
2. You shall confess your sins at least once a year.
3. You shall receive the sacrament of the Eucharist at least during the Easter season.

4. You shall observe the days of fasting and abstinence established by the Church.
5. You shall help to provide for the needs of the Church.

(*Compendium*, p. 193 [Appendix B]; see CCC, nos. 2041-2043)

PART II

 ummarizing from the *Catechism of the Catholic Church*, this second part of *Essentials for Christian Living* contains

- What the faith is (the twelve articles of the Creed)
- What the faith gives (the seven sacraments)
- What the faith requires (the Ten Commandments)

WHAT IS THE FAITH?
(THE CREED)

Faith means to believe that God loves us, and to believe in God who speaks.

"In accordance with an ancient tradition, already attested to by Saint Ambrose, it is also customary to reckon the articles of the Creed as *twelve*, thus symbolizing the fullness of the apostolic faith by the number of the apostles" (CCC, no. 191).

1. God the Creator
2. The Son of the living God
3. The Savior
4. The Redeemer
5. The Risen One
6. The Ascension into heaven
7. The Judgment
8. The Holy Spirit
9. The Catholic Church
10. The Sanctifier
11. The Resurrection in Christ
12. The life everlasting in Christ

1. God the Creator

**I believe in God,
the Father almighty,
creator of heaven and earth.**

"'In the beginning God created the heavens and the earth' (Gn 1:1). Holy Scripture begins with these solemn words" (CCC, no. 279).

"The Credo begins with God the *Father*, for the Father is the first divine person of the Most Holy Trinity" (CCC, no. 198).

"Starting from movement, becoming, contingency, and the world's order and beauty, one can come to a knowledge of God as the origin and the end of the universe" (CCC, no. 32).

2. The Son of the Living God

I believe in Jesus Christ, his only Son, our Lord.

"For God so loved the world that he gave his only Son, so that everyone who believes in him might not perish but might have eternal life" (Jn 3:16).

"Moved by the grace of the Holy Spirit and drawn by the Father, we believe in Jesus and confess: 'You are the Christ, the Son of the living God' (Mt 16:16)" (CCC, no. 424).

"This is my chosen Son; listen to him" (Lk 9:35).

3. The Savior

He was conceived
by the power of the Holy Spirit
and born of the Virgin Mary.

"The Holy Spirit, 'the Lord, the giver of Life,' is sent to sanctify the womb of the Virgin Mary" (CCC, no. 485).

"Belief in the true Incarnation of the Son of God is the distinctive sign of Christian faith" (CCC, no. 463).

"He became truly man while remaining truly God. Jesus Christ is true God and true man" (CCC, no. 464).

4. The Redeemer

He suffered under Pontius Pilate, was crucified, died, and was buried.

"In the fifteenth year of the reign of Tiberius Caesar, when Pontius Pilate was governor of Judea, and Herod was tetrarch of Galilee . . ." (Lk 3:1).

"They cried out, 'Take him away, take him away! Crucify him!'" (Jn 19:15).

"It is truly the Son of God made man who died and was buried" (CCC, no. 629).

5. The Risen One

He descended into hell.
On the third day he rose again.

"The descent into hell brings the Gospel message of salvation to complete fulfillment . . . the spread of Christ's redemptive work to all men of all times and all places . . ." (CCC, no. 634).

"Why do you seek the living one among the dead? He is not here, but he has been raised" (Lk 24:5-6).

"And if Christ has not been raised, then empty [too] is our preaching; empty, too, your faith" (1 Cor 15:14).

6. The Ascension into Heaven

He ascended into heaven and is seated at the right hand of the Father.

"So then the Lord Jesus, after he spoke to them, was taken up into heaven and took his seat at the right hand of God" (Mk 16:19).

"Christ's ascension marks the definitive entrance of Jesus' humanity into God's heavenly domain, whence he will come again" (CCC, no. 665).

"Jesus Christ, the head of the Church, precedes us into the Father's glorious kingdom so that we, the members of his Body, may live in the hope of one day being with him for ever" (CCC, no. 666).

7. The Judgment

He will come again to judge the living and the dead.

"For this is why Christ died and came to life, that he might be Lord of both the dead and the living" (Rom 14:9).

"When he comes at the end of time to judge the living and the dead, the glorious Christ will reveal the secret disposition of hearts and will render to each man according to his works and according to his acceptance or refusal of grace" (CCC, no. 682).

"On the last day Jesus will say: 'Truly I say to you, as you did it to one of the least of these my brethren, you did it to me' (Mt 25:40)" (CCC, no. 678).

8. The Holy Spirit

I believe in the Holy Spirit.

"On the day of Pentecost . . . Christ's Passover is fulfilled in the outpouring of the Holy Spirit" (CCC, no. 731).

"The love of God has been poured out into our hearts through the holy Spirit that has been given to us" (Rom 5:5).

"To believe in the Holy Spirit is to profess that the Holy Spirit is one of the persons of the Holy Trinity, consubstantial with the Father and the Son" (CCC, no. 685).

9. The Catholic Church

I believe in the holy catholic Church, the communion of saints.

"Hence the universal Church is seen to be 'a people brought into unity from the unity of the Father, the Son, and the Holy Spirit'" (CCC, no. 810, quoting *Lumen Gentium*, no. 4).

"The Church in this world is the sacrament of salvation, the sign and the instrument of the communion of God and men" (CCC, no. 780).

"Particular Churches are fully catholic through their communion with one of them, the Church of Rome 'which presides in charity'" (CCC, no. 834, quoting St. Ignatius of Antioch).

10. The Sanctifier

I believe in the forgiveness of sins.

"Those who are well do not need a physician, but the sick do" (Mt 9:12).

"The Apostles' Creed associates faith in the forgiveness of sins not only with faith in the Holy Spirit. . . . The risen Christ conferred on [his apostles] his own divine power to forgive sins: 'Receive the Holy Spirit. If you forgive the sins of any, they are forgiven; if you retain the sins of any, they are retained' (Jn 20:22-23)" (CCC, no. 976).

11. The Resurrection in Christ

I believe in the resurrection of the body.

"I am the resurrection and the life" (Jn 11:25).

"We firmly believe, and hence we hope that, just as Christ is truly risen from the dead and lives for ever, so after death the righteous will live for ever with the risen Christ . . ." (CCC, no. 989).

"Every action of yours, every thought, should be those of one who expects to die before the day is out" (CCC, no. 1014, quoting *The Imitation of Christ*).

12. The Life Everlasting in Christ

I believe in the life everlasting.

"The Christian who unites his own death to that of Jesus views it as a step towards him and an entrance into everlasting life" (CCC, no. 1020).

"Whoever believes in the Son has eternal life" (Jn 3:36).

"If for this life only we have hoped in Christ, we are the most pitiable people of all" (1 Cor 15:19).

_____

_____

_____

_____

Amen

"The Creed, like the last book of the Bible, ends with the Hebrew word amen. . . . The Church likewise ends her prayers with 'Amen'" (CCC, no. 1061).

"The 'Amen' may express both God's faithfulness towards us and our trust in him" (CCC, no. 1062).

"To believe is to say 'Amen' to God's words, promises and commandments" (CCC, no. 1064).

What Does the Faith Give? (The Sacraments)

"By dying he destroyed our death; by rising he restored our life" (*Roman Missal*, from the Easter preface).

"Christ now lives and acts in and with his Church . . . through the sacraments"
(CCC, no. 1076).

"The sacraments are efficacious signs of grace, instituted by Christ and entrusted to the Church, by which divine life is dispensed to us" (CCC, no. 1131).

1. The Sacrament of Baptism

"Go, therefore, and make disciples of all nations, baptizing them in the name of the Father, and of the Son, and of the holy Spirit" (Mt 28:19).

"Holy Baptism is the basis of the whole Christian life" (CCC, no. 1213).

"Baptism is birth into the new life in Christ" (CCC, no. 1277).

2. The Sacrament of Confirmation or Chrismation

"Confirmation perfects Baptismal grace" (CCC, no. 1316).

"The effect of the sacrament of Confirmation is the special outpouring of the Holy Spirit as once granted to the apostles on the day of Pentecost" (CCC, no. 1302).

"Confirmation, like Baptism, imprints a spiritual mark or indelible character on the Christian's soul" (CCC, no. 1317).

3. The Sacrament of the Eucharist

"I am the living bread that came down from heaven; whoever eats this bread will live forever" (Jn 6:51).

"The Eucharist is the heart and summit of the Church's life" (CCC, no. 1407).

"At the Last Supper, on the night he was betrayed, our Savior instituted the Eucharistic sacrifice of his Body and Blood" (CCC, no. 1323, quoting *Sacrosanctum Concilium*, no. 47).

4. The Sacrament of Penance or Reconciliation

"Child, your sins are forgiven" (Mk 2:5).

"The Sacrament of Penance is a whole consisting in three actions of the penitent and the priest's absolution. The penitent's acts are repentance, confession . . . and the intention to make reparation and do works of reparation" (CCC, no. 1491).

_____

_____

_____

_____

5. The Sacrament of the Anointing of the Sick

"Illness and suffering have always been among the gravest problems confronted in human life" (CCC, no. 1500).

"The Sacrament of Anointing of the Sick has as its purpose the conferral of a special grace on the Christian experiencing the difficulties inherent in the condition of grave illness or old age" (CCC, no. 1527).

6. The Sacrament of Holy Orders

"Holy Orders is the sacrament through which the mission entrusted by Christ to his apostles continues to be exercised in the Church until the end of time: thus it is the sacrament of apostolic ministry. It includes three degrees: episcopate, presbyterate, and diaconate" (CCC, no. 1536).

"Ordination imprints an indelible sacramental character" (CCC, no. 1597).

7. The Sacrament of Matrimony

"God who created man out of love also calls him to love—the fundamental and innate vocation of every human being. . . . Since God created him man and woman, their mutual love becomes an image of the absolute and unfailing love with which God loves man" (CCC, no. 1604).

"The love of the spouses requires, of its very nature, the unity and indissolubility of the spouses' community of persons, which embraces their entire life: 'so they are no longer two, but one flesh'" (CCC, no. 1644, quoting Mt 19:6 and Gn 2:24).

WHAT DOES THE FAITH REQUIRE? (THE COMMANDMENTS)

"Christian, recognize your dignity and, now that you share in God's own nature, do not return to your former base condition by sinning" (CCC, no. 1691, quoting St. Leo the Great).

"The way of Christ 'leads to life'; a contrary way 'leads to destruction.' The Gospel parable of the *two ways* remains ever present in the catechesis of the Church; it shows the importance of moral decisions for our salvation . . ." (CCC, no. 1696).

"'Teacher, what good deed must I do, to have eternal life?' To the young man who asked this question, Jesus answers first by invoking the necessity to recognize God as the 'One there is who is good,' as the supreme Good and the source of all good. Then Jesus tells him: 'If you would enter life, keep the commandments'" (CCC, no. 2052).

1.

I am the LORD your God: you shall not have strange gods before me.

"The first commandment summons man to believe in God, to hope in him, and to love him above all else" (CCC, no. 2134).

"You shall love the LORD, your God, with all your heart, and with all your soul, and with all your strength" (Dt 6:5).

"The duty to offer God authentic worship concerns man both as an individual and as a social being" (CCC, no. 2136).

2.

You shall not take the name of the LORD your God in vain.

"The second commandment *prescribes respect for the Lord's name*" (CCC, no. 2142).

"Respect for his name is an expression of the respect owed to the mystery of God himself and to the whole sacred reality it evokes" (CCC, no. 2144).

"Blasphemy is directly opposed to the second commandment" (CCC, no. 2148).

3.

Remember to keep holy the Lord's Day.

"The Church celebrates the day of Christ's Resurrection on the 'eighth day,' Sunday, which is rightly called the Lord's Day" (CCC, no. 2191)

"Those Christians who have leisure should be mindful of their brethren. . . . Sunday is traditionally consecrated by Christian piety to good works and humble service of the sick, the infirm, and the elderly" (CCC, no. 2186).

4.

Honor your father and your mother.

"He went down with them and came to Nazareth, and was obedient to them" (Lk 2:51).

"God has willed that, after him, we should honor our parents to whom we owe life and who have handed on to us the knowledge of God" (CCC, no. 2197).

"Respecting this commandment provides, along with spiritual fruits, temporal fruits of peace and prosperity" (CCC, no. 2200).

5.

You shall not kill.

"The fifth commandment forbids the intentional destruction of human life" (CCC, no. 2307).

"Every human life, from the moment of conception until death, is sacred because the human person has been willed for its own sake in the image and likeness of the living and holy God" (CCC, no. 2319).

"The murder of a human being is gravely contrary to the dignity of the person and the holiness of the Creator" (CCC, no. 2320).

6.

You shall not commit adultery.

"Adultery, divorce, polygamy, and free union are grave offenses against the dignity of marriage" (CCC, no. 2400).

"Whoever wants to remain faithful to his baptismal promises and resist temptations will want to adopt the *means* for doing so: self-knowledge, practice of an ascesis . . . , obedience to God's commandments, exercise of the moral virtues, and fidelity to prayer" (CCC, no. 2340).

7.

You shall not steal.

"The seventh commandment enjoins the practice of justice and charity in the administration of earthly goods and the fruits of men's labor" (CCC, no. 2451).

"Every manner of taking and using another's property unjustly is contrary to the seventh commandment" (CCC, no. 2454).

"Neither thieves nor the greedy . . . will inherit the kingdom of God" (1 Cor 6:10).

8.

You shall not bear false witness against your neighbor.

"To his disciples Jesus teaches the unconditional love of truth: 'Let what you say be simply 'Yes or No' (Mt 5:37)" (CCC, no. 2466).

"The eighth commandment forbids misrepresenting the truth in our relations with others" (CCC, no. 2464).

"The Christian is not to 'be ashamed of testifying to our Lord' (2 Tim 1:8) in deed and word. Martyrdom is the supreme witness given to the truth of the faith" (CCC, no. 2506).

9.

You shall not covet your neighbor's wife.

"The ninth commandment warns against lust or carnal concupiscence" (CCC, no. 2529).

"The struggle against carnal lust involves purifying the heart and practicing temperance" (CCC, no. 2530).

"Do not follow your base desires, but restrain your appetites" (CCC, no. 1809, quoting Sir 18:30).

10.

You shall not covet your neighbor's goods.

"The tenth commandment forbids avarice arising from a passion for riches and their attendant power" (CCC, no. 2552).

"Detachment from riches is necessary for entering the Kingdom of heaven. 'Blessed are the poor in spirit'" (CCC, no. 2556).

"'I want to see God' expresses the true desire of man. Thirst for God is quenched by the water of eternal life" (CCC, no. 2557; see Jn 4:14).

CONCLUSION

ssentials for Christian Living concludes with a page from the evangelist Matthew. The text, when it is read and reflected upon, reveals and leads to a philosophy of life that is an encounter with the person of Christ, an essential part of the life of a Christian.

> When the Son of Man comes in his glory, and all the angels with him, he will sit upon his glorious throne, and all the nations will be assembled before him. And he will separate them one from another, as a shepherd separates the sheep from the goats. He will place the sheep on his right and the goats on his left. Then the king will say to those on his right, "Come, you who are blessed by my Father. Inherit the kingdom prepared for you from the foundation of the world. For I was hungry and you gave me food, I was thirsty and you gave me drink, a stranger and you welcomed me, naked and you clothed me, ill and you cared for

me, in prison and you visited me." Then the righteous will answer him and say, "Lord, when did we see you hungry and feed you, or thirsty and give you drink? When did we see you a stranger and welcome you, or naked and clothe you? When did we see you ill or in prison, and visit you?" And the king will say to them in reply, "Amen, I say to you, whatever you did for one of these least brothers of mine, you did for me." Then he will say to those on his left, "Depart from me, you accursed, into the eternal fire prepared for the devil and his angels. For I was hungry and you gave me no food, I was thirsty and you gave me no drink, a stranger and you gave me no welcome, naked and you gave me no clothing, ill and in prison, and you did not care for me." Then they will answer and say, "Lord, when did we see you hungry or thirsty or a stranger or naked or ill or prison, and not minister to your needs?" He will answer them, "Amen, I say to you, what you did not do for one of these least ones, you did not do for me." And these will go off to eternal punishment, but the righteous to eternal life. (Mt 25:31-46)

SUBJECT INDEX